"Le [Me] Stop You Right There"

And…

28 Other Lines every CEO, Manager, and Supervisor Should Know

Pamela D. Straker, Ph.D.

NEW YORK

"Let Me Stop You Right There"

And... 28 Other Lines every CEO, Manager, and Supervisor Should Know

by Pamela D. Straker, Ph.D.

© 2011 Pamela D. Straker, Ph.D. All rights reserved.

ISBN 978-160037-695-5 (paperback)

Library of Congress Control Number 2010929328

Published by:

MORGAN JAMES PUBLISHING
1225 Franklin Ave. Ste 325
Garden City, NY 11530-1693
Toll Free 800-485-4943
www.MorganJamesPublishing.com

Illustrator:
Adam L. Weaver
adam@adamweaver.net

Interior Design by:
Bonnie Bushman
bbushman@bresnan.net

In an effort to support local communities, raise awareness and funds, Morgan James Publishing donates one percent of all book sales for the life of each book to Habitat for Humanity.
Get involved today, visit
www.HelpHabitatForHumanity.org.

Acknowledgments

I thank my family and friends, all of whom contributed to this effort in one way or another.

My four grandparents, Fitzherbert, Miriam, Milton and Enid led the way with their visionary spirits, tackling first generation experiences in the USA. The wisdom they shared with me has been invaluable. I thank my parents Milton, who actually loved to write, and Dorothy, who taught me how. My sisters, D'jvonne and Allyson, and my brother-in-law Robert continue to enrich my life with their sense of what is truly important. My nieces Ariel and Chelsea are also my inspiration because they represent the future and all that can be. Dolores, your spirit continues to inspire me and I know you are an angel protecting me from afar. Brian, your tenacity and your support have buoyed me at some of my most difficult professional moments.

To my friends Robert, Phyllis, Charles, Gloria, Jackie, Peter, Jim, Alexis, Jan, and Cheryl who have read, listened, supported, and guided, I am eternally thankful. Additionally, I am thankful for all of the interactions I've had with bosses, staff, board members, funders, and clients. These interactions, whether positive, negative, easy, or challenging contributed to developing the lines included in this book. Special thanks to Gail and Linda without whom this project would not have been completed.

Finally, thank you to everyone who reads this book. May you have a chuckle as you recognize the actions of others or of yourself as you read on!

Contents

Acknowledgments iii

Foreword ix

The Lines

1. "Let me stop you right there." 1

2. "Your personal life is interfering with
   the functioning of the office." 5

3. "And your point is? or "Where are you
   going with this?" 9

4. "You've created this mess, now how
   do you propose to clean it up?" 13

5. "If only I could." 17

6. "Oh dear, that is far too much
   information." 21

7. "Is there something I can do about
    it right now?" 25

8. "What do you think you should do?" or
    "What do you think should be done?".............29

9. "And you thought that action would
    accomplish what?"...33

10. "Let me think about that and discuss
    it with you in our next supervisory
    session." or "I can respond to that by
    tomorrow at 12 noon." 37

11. "Thank you for not sharing." 41

12. "Wow!" or "Gee!" or "How interesting!"
    or "Oh my!" 45

13. "So what I hear you saying is…?" 49

14. "I am having great difficulty hearing you
    right now. Perhaps we should talk later."........53

15. "What is the worst possible outcome
    if we try something new?"...............................57

16. "Silence"… the sound of crickets....................61

17. "I wish you and your family well at
    this time and am sorry for your loss." 65

18. "You do have choices." 69

19. "Let's discuss it over coffee, tea,
    or lunch." 73

20. "If this continues, I will have
    no recourse…". 77

21. "Your next vacation is scheduled
    for when?" 81

22. "Your employment has been terminated." 85

23. "Actually…no." 89

24. "Get over it!" 93

25. "Stay in your lane." 97

26. "Bring it on." 101

27. "I've stayed too long at the fair." 105

28. "Requiem for An Assassin…
    Light reading anyone?" 109

29. "In the end, the truth will come out." 113

Foreword

Have you ever noticed that great CEOs, managers and other people in charge always seem to know exactly what to say in every situation? It is as if they have a storehouse of information and lines always available to them.

This book is designed to give you lines associated with scenarios you might experience at your organization. The lines and the scenes in which they may be used are in some instances interchangeable and/or useful for other scenes you may experience.

The only requirement in reading this book is that you smile when you recognize something that fits a situation you have encountered in the past or anticipate you will encounter. Enjoy!

Line 1:

Let Me Stop You Right There.

1. The Line:

"Let Me Stop You Right There."

The Scene:

Your highest functioning employee is on a tear, bulldozing others, "leaving bodies at the side of the road." While he gets a tremendous amount accomplished, it is at great cost to the team's morale. He barks orders, punishes through passive aggressive acts, appears to be vindictive in his actions, and is moody. Most recently, he has used a commanding tone when speaking with you...as if he is giving you orders. You schedule to meet with him and in that meeting; he begins to direct you again. You say "Let me stop you right there."

What Could It All Mean?

Sometimes your best people are so caught up in achieving their goals, they lose sight of the impact they are having on others. They have received positive feedback for "getting the job done" and have possibly bought into the "by any means necessary" way of thinking. Now they even think they can tell <u>you</u> what to do. Your statement will probably surprise them since they have been "on a roll" and are not expecting it. Another possibility is that these individuals may have outgrown a "middle level" position and may need to try their hand at running the whole show themselves. They may need to find the position that gives them all of the power (and responsibility) for which they seem to yearn. Often they learn that they must function differently if they are totally in charge. In any event you must stop them from damaging the morale of your staff when they are working in your shop.

Line 2:

Your Personal Life Is Interfering With The Functioning Of The Office.

"Your Personal Life Is Interfering With The Functioning Of The Office."

The Scene:

You're lying on the beach sipping a Pina Colada...just beginning to forget the name of the company, program, or organization you run. You get the dreaded e-mail. You forgot to totally disconnect! You read it and find out that your assistant is requesting additional vacation days, not related to any life or death situation. This means you'll return to no assistant and a blistering amount of unfinished work, in addition to tackling the new projects you'd already scheduled to begin after your vacation. You recall the painstaking way in which you organized six months in advance, requesting schedules for coverage of the office and schedules for vacation, while informing your assistant that you would need her when you returned. You e-mail back that this request isn't working for you. She e-mails back that she has the days and "she doesn't see what the problem is." You e-mail back, "Your personal life is interfering with the function of the office," and turn off your PDA.

What Could It All Mean?

At the end of the day, you probably need to explore whether your assistant is the best fit for the job. She is there to assist you after all. Recognize that her behavior may actually be a manipulation on her part to avoid doing the work, which will force you to face the pressure of returning to your office without the help you need. There are many examples of people in management positions who suffer for long periods of time with support staff who do not provide the service for which they were hired. This type of situation could be noted to happen when clear boundaries have not been established or when one inherits someone else's staff person.

Your line encapsulates the situation and while on vacation, no more needs to be said. The weight of the decision is now where it belongs, on the assistant who is ducking out on her responsibilities. She may take the extra days and require you to hire a temp, which will result in her being disciplined with at least a memo to her personnel file or, if enough documentation exists, fired. Or, she may not take the extra days. Whatever happens, the manner in which she discharges her responsibilities warrants further review.

Line 3:
Where Are You Going With THIS?

"And Your Point Is?" Or "Where Are You Going With THIS?"

The Scene:

You are running a meeting for your direct reports. You are discussing the functions assigned to the assistant who has done an excellent job for every person attending the meeting. One of your direct reports says, "You know he's gay." You are amazed and really do not understand why this person felt the need to explore the assistant's sexuality. Further, you recognize that anything you say could result in your assuming responsibility for introducing or further discussing the topic. Your only recourse appears to be to punt the discussion back and so you say, "And your point is?" or "Where are you (versus we) going with this?"

What Could It All Mean?

Interestingly, people often feel comfortable in taking liberties with personal information regarding others. In this instance, the person choosing to discuss the life of the assistant may feel he is adding a sense of interest to the meeting...I prefer to call it gossip...that others may pick up on. Continuing the conversation, in any way traps you in that you are now involved in discussing the intimate affairs of others. Moreover, you are being observed doing this so that, should one of your other direct reports need to share something of a personal nature (there are times when this is appropriate), they will not do so because you cannot be trusted to keep confidences.

Line 4:
You've Created This Mess, Now How Do You Propose To Clean It Up?

"You've Created This Mess, Now How Do You Propose To Clean It Up?"

The Scene:

A valued member of the management team who is capable of highly productive and creative solutions, is acting inappropriately...repeatedly arriving late to work, requiring others to fill in for him, returning late from lunch, resulting in others looking for him, etc. One of the team members who backs him up finally calls you in exasperation requesting that something be done. You remember the very tactful way in which this employee's references tried to describe this aspect of his performance, while lauding his talents. "He has an independent spirit," a reference said. You chose to interpret that as his being willing to get things done without assistance…something we all dream of! You know that this individual is accustomed to being praised for his brilliance and you recognize that he has likely never been "called on the carpet" for his actions. Even his current team members have developed excuses for him until now. What could you possibly say to get him to get a grip…light bulb moment…give him the grip! You call a meeting with the "independent" team member and you say, "You've created a mess, now how do you propose to clean it up?!"

What Could It All Mean?

This could also apply to the person who is a high performer, but feels that this entitles him to special privileges. It might be that you, as his supervisor, and others before you, have even admired him and supported him in his "out of the box" thinking and implementation. Hence, he now has the "they really can't do with out me" or "let them eat cake" attitude. Your challenge is to manage his ego while allowing the organization to benefit from his brilliance. This is best done by setting clear limits and bringing him into the position to rectify his mistakes. He should be the one to apologize or otherwise makeup with his teammates. I would be remiss if I did not mention a couple of other items in reference to this line.

First, recognize that there are some people who, as the co-workers of the aforementioned person, cannot tolerate highly competent and creative people. They feel the need to "rain on the parade" of those who are quick and efficient. You will have to be careful if this type of person brings the complaint. He or she may be dealing with his or her own jealousy.

Second, avoid the mistaken belief of thinking that a person who has been described as brilliant will be so in your setting. This can result in prematurely implying that special privileges will be allowed resulting in the person taking liberties. Care should be taken in assessing all staff whether they are reportedly brilliant or not.

Line 5:
If Only I Could...

"Please, Just One More Ticket."

5. The Line:

"If Only I Could."

The Scene:

Your office has been invited to attend a special event that features a major star from the motion picture industry. You offer tickets to your staff to show appreciation for their hard work. The number of tickets is limited and you want to be fair about who attends from the organization. One of your staff requests to have their "significant other" attend the event, too. You say "If only I could."

What Could It All Mean?

There is an art to saying no to people's requests. An important part of the art is to do so without malice and without leaving the person feeling decimated. This is particularly important when you'd like the person to continue to feel appreciated. It is best to make statements short and sweet to avoid awkward moments. Sometimes it might work to anticipate situations that might lead to your having to say no. In this instance, you might have said in advance, "Complimentary tickets to this event are for staff only. We are unable to include family or friends. If you wish to purchase tickets…"

Line 6:
OH DEAR,
That Is Far Too
Much Information.

6. The Line:

"OH DEAR, That Is Far Too Much Information."

The Scene:

A staff person has returned after a prolonged absence during which they had an elective surgical procedure. You see them and politely indicate that you hope they are recovering well. They launch into an extensive discussion during which they indicate how many stitches, precisely where, how it felt, etc. Even when you shift focus slightly to suggest discomfort with the discussion, the hint is not taken. When you are being introduced to the person's internal organs, you finally say, "Oh dear, that is far too much information."

What Could It All Mean?

There are those who believe that the discussion of their own personal or physical information makes them socially open in a positive way and is helpful in establishing intimate relationships. Some like to wear their medical history like a badge. They are unaware of the discomfort it may cause others and of the likely inappropriateness of its discussion in a work context and particularly with you. Your line has clearly let them know that "you are not the one" for this level of discussion and should be followed by removing yourself from the person's presence. A simple, "I've got to get back to my office" will suffice. Needless to say, there are instances when staff should indicate their capacity or incapacity to work. There are also instances when a level of intimacy has been established making a deeper discussion of physical details appropriate. You are in control of your participation in discussions of this sort.

Line 7:

Is There Something

I Can Do About It

RIGHT NOW?

7. The Line:

"Is There Something I Can Do About It RIGHT NOW?"

The Scene:

You are trying to meet a deadline on a report you are writing. It is the end of the day. Your office door is closed as you finally cull out the time to focus on your document. Suddenly, you are interrupted by a senior manager who has ignored your assistant's pleas to allow her to contact you to determine whether you should be interrupted for the matter. The manager knocks and opens the door (without your "come in" response) and begins with, "This is urgent!!!" Before your manager can say anything further you say, "Is there something I can do about the situation right now? If not, I'd like to discuss it in our meeting scheduled for tomorrow."

What Could It All Mean?

One of the most interesting things within an office setting is to observe the impact a closed door has on your management team. For some, the closed door is a signal that they have been permanently cut off from communication with you. They must find a way in!! Others have difficulty with an executive assistant establishing the boundary at your door. They are, after all, superior to your executive assistant! For others the closed door suggests that you have established a priority that does not involve them or that their priorities might not come before any that you or anyone else in the organization has established. Whichever fits your team member, you must reinforce your right and responsibility to take appropriate charge of your time in the office. Unless the "urgent situation" must be resolved by you at that moment, you should hold firm on completing your own work and request that the team member close the door upon leaving your office.

Line 8:

What Do <u>YOU</u> Think Should Be Done?

"What Do You Think You Should Do?" or "What Do You Think Should Be Done?"

The Scene:

An experienced, senior member of the team seeks your advice on resolving a situation within her area of responsibility, (i.e. her staff has been delinquent in submitting their schedules). You wonder why she is asking you since she is so highly competent in the execution of her duties. While you could easily give her the resolution from your perspective, you recognize the need to help her grow in the area of independent functioning. You are also aware that recently, a great deal of your time with her has been spent discussing things you know she is capable of handling. You say, "What do you think you should do?" or "What do you think should be done?"

What Could It All Mean?

The number of highly capable people who show no independence of thought in areas where they should is remarkable. It is your job as a "person in charge" to mentor that aspect of their performance. Think carefully about whether your management style has actually encouraged people to avoid handling situations or making decisions independently. Encourage people to manage their responsibilities; otherwise, you will wind up doing their jobs and wondering how this happened.

Line 9:
And You Thought
That Action
Would Accomplish
WHAT?

"We Know What To Do About This Situation!"

9. The Line:

"And You Thought That Action Would Accomplish WHAT?"

The Scene:

As the long-term leader of an organization, you and your management team have successfully dealt with the various urgent situations confronting the organization, with little assistance from board members. In response to a provocative letter sent by the union representing a faction of your staff, the board responds without informing you and without any information from you or the members of your team. The situation with the union implodes and the board seeks to blame you and the team for the disaster and for what ensues thereafter. When you meet with your board, you say, "And you thought that action would accomplish what?"

What Could It All Mean?

Actions of the sort described in this scenario should be looked at for what they are...the potential beginning of the end. When there is a breach in cohesiveness promoted by the governing body of your organization, it is probably best that you take quick action to secure your future elsewhere or, at the very least, know that the end is near. Many excellent leaders have had to contend with inexperienced or grandiose board members who, in the interest of projecting themselves as being in charge, take actions that can destroy all that has been accomplished. Once the "power" of feeling in charge is felt by these individuals, it is unlikely that they will take responsibility for their less than professional actions. If you find yourself in this situation, your most productive course of action is to assess the possibilities for reconciliation and, in the absence of these, to pursue a timely exit.

Line 10:

I Can Respond To That By Tomorrow At 12 Noon.

"Let me think about that and discuss it with you in our next supervisory session." or "I can respond to that by tomorrow at 12 noon."

The Scene:

A member of the management team approaches you with the proposal that he convert to a four-day work week. You basically believe in flexible hours, know that this person is a responsible worker, and think that this may be a way to reward him for his dedication and commitment. You do have concerns about the precedence such an arrangement sets, the capacity to schedule face-to-face meetings in the future, and other human resources issues you may not be thinking of in the 30 seconds you've considered it so far. You say, "Let me think about that and discuss it with you in our next supervisory session."

What Could It All Mean?

Sometimes, a pause in the action is needed. This line is the greatest pause button ever. It allows you time to think about the topic or to think through the situation. People in charge are often perceived to be responsible for immediate answers, and, by the way, tend to like to give immediate answers because they lean toward efficiency of action. Just a comment on this particular line—it should not be used too often nor should the period of time the person must wait for a response be interminable. Some people in charge use this to actually "make the process painful" by dragging out the response time or passive aggressively never responding to what was asked. It probably is best, if possible, to say how long you plan to think about it and to give a clear response within the designated time frame.

Line 11:
Thank You For NOT Sharing.

"...And Last But Not Least, We Are Almost Out Of Staples and Paperclips."

11. The Line:

"Thank You For NOT Sharing."

The Scene:

One of your most responsible managers has the habit of discussing with you every detail of every issue he manages. Though you have indirectly and directly assured him that you are confident regarding his decision making, he continues to give you the details. Recently, he has taken to interrupting your flow of activity to tell you about things "he wanted to tell you because he thought you should know." You finally say to him, "Thank-you for not sharing."

What Could It All Mean?

Sometimes your direct reports feel they need more of your attention and sometimes they feel that their priorities should command more of your attention. Sometimes interrupting you with details is designed to reinforce in their own minds the importance of their roles. After all, the things they are dealing with are "things the CEO should know about." In the best of all worlds, you have provided them with a time when the "real issues you should know about" as you see them, can be defined and discussed. Once you have done that, you must let people carry their own burdens. Otherwise, you will be less able to carry out your own goals and activities. Your managers should know that not sharing is often the correct choice.

Line 12:

WOW! or GEE!
or How Interesting!
or Oh My!

12. The Line:

"WOW!" or "GEE!" or "How Interesting!" or "Oh My!"

The Scene:

You are on your way to an important meeting and a group of assistants are gathered in the conference room you are passing, discussing fabric samples for the conference room chairs. You have delegated the decision to them and the professional designer from a major show house. You truly have no skill in choosing colors or textures. Your assistant calls to you to show you the multitude of possibilities the designer has just offered. You briefly join the group, citing your need to continue on to a meeting and you say, "Wow!, how interesting!" , followed by, "I know you guys will do a great job…I do have to run."

What Could It All Mean?

There are times when you don't wish to add to a conversation and yet you don't wish to turn the speaker off. You are using verbal place holders that, while not putting you in the position of extending the discussion, suggest that you have heard what the speaker said. There are any number of these, but they should be used judiciously otherwise people will begin to feel that you just don't care about what they are saying. These are particularly useful for the discussions you hear walking by a group and, being signaled to join in, do so but know nothing about what is being discussed. Your comment is made and you then resume the direction in which you were headed. Your staff is left feeling that you at least took the time to give them a little attention.

Line 13:

So What I Hear You Saying Is...?

13. The Line:

"So What I Hear You Saying Is...?"

The Scene:

At a meeting of your directors, a participant gives a long rambling complaint about an organizational process designed to improve productivity. After a significant period of frustration on the part of the other participants and attempts to have her clarify her position, you intercede with what your understanding of what the director is attempting to communicate. You say, "So what I hear you saying is...?"

What Could It All Mean?

Helping others to clarify their positions and complaints is an important part of the role of a leader. Sometimes, in the heat of a meeting, a discussant will lose focus and be drawn into unrelated details. Indeed, there are those who have a proclivity for obfuscating or muddying their own point. It becomes the role of the person leading the group or meeting to get back on target. The goal is to assist the group in focusing upon solutions rather than upon a complaint and/or further unneeded attempts to clarify what is being presented. Skillful clarification results in much more productive meetings.

Line 14:
I Am Having Great Difficulty Hearing You
RIGHT NOW,
Perhaps We Should Talk
LATER...

14. The Line:

"I Am Having Great Difficulty Hearing You RIGHT NOW. Perhaps We Should Talk LATER."

The Scene:

You are supervising someone who generally has great enthusiasm about her position and about how the department should be run. On a given day, however, she mishandles an interaction with a client. You call her aside and attempt to speak to her about the situation whereupon she begins to yell, curse, and act in an inappropriate manner. You say, "I am having great difficulty hearing you right now. Perhaps we should talk later." And you leave her or indicate by standing and walking to the door that she should leave.

What Could It All Mean?

To conclude that the behavior of this staff person is unacceptable goes without saying. Dealing with the behavior effectively is more of a challenge. First, if a productive direction is desired, it is important to cool the interaction by immediately disengaging from the battle. Often, people in charge seek to "win the battle" when instead it is critical to determine whether there is a war being waged. Given the volatility of the staff person's response, other issues impacting upon the workplace may be of concern. As soon as is possible after the incident, perhaps the following day, it is important to request that the staff person meet with you. In this meeting your goal is to allow an explanation on the part of the staff person while setting limits. While you want to give the staff person an opportunity to explain the outburst and/or to make amends, you also must make clear that the behavior will not be tolerated and that you must take some action. You may decide to write a supervisory warning note to be sent to the staff member with a copy maintained in your supervision file. If this has happened on more than one occasion, you may decide to involve your human resources office, particularly if you feel that this staff person may ultimately be fired.

The decision to meet with the staff person is also predicated upon there being no indication of physical threat to you or anyone else. Statements of intent to harm should be considered seriously. In such instances, organizational protocols for the management of violent persons should be followed. As a manager, you should have a person (i.e. assistant, colleague) who, upon hearing certain code words, will call security and/or the police.

Line 15:
What Is The Worst
Possible Outcome
If We Try Something
NEW?

"But It's Always Been Done This Way"

"What Is The Worst Possible Outcome If We Try Something NEW?"

The Scene:

You are conducting a series of meetings in which you are outlining a new strategic direction. You have presented the data to support the change in focus and have engaged all but one of your direct reports. At every possible opportunity, she talks about "The way it has always been done..." or inserts "That plan may not work because..." This individual is very meticulous with the details of her work but often robs the energy of the group with her negative response to change. At one of the meetings critical to moving plans forward, she again bashes the new idea. You finally say, "What is the worst possible outcome if we try something new?"

What Could It All Mean?

There are people for whom change is truly threatening to their sense of stability and "sameness." They have made a "name" for themselves by knowing every rule and being able to recite them. Generally, they may be controlling types who also enjoy identifying when others make a mistake. The danger they present in the work place is that, while they may be correct about the rules, they stifle all innovation that might lead to the organization becoming a better place. Your line forces them to confront the way in which they are perceived and to confront what may be their fears about the situation at hand. You are likely to have to use this line more than once if you have such an individual on your team. In the meeting in which you employ this line, be sure you don't allow too much time on the worst case scenario. If you feel it should be addressed, have a separate time to capture the actions in the event of a failure. Don't allow the "wet blanket" to take away the energy of the meeting with a long protracted discussion of the negatives. It is important to monitor the situation if this person is in the position of supervising staff. They are often threatened by others who are creative, interesting and innovative people. You may find that they prevent the very people you want in the organization from being hired. As well, they may be responsible for major dissatisfaction among younger, innovative staff members.

Line 16:

Silence...
The Sound Of Crickets.

16. The Line:

"Silence"...
The Sound Of
Crickets

The Scene:

You are in a meeting with your supervisors in which one decides to speak negatively about another supervisor criticizing them for their absence from the meeting. The supervisor who is absent has a life threatening illness, the nature of which has been shared with all. Upon being reminded of this, the callous supervisor states, "We all have problems." You recall the way in which this person has criticized others and has a reputation for this type of behavior. You also remember supporting this person through periods when he was confronted with difficult personal situations. Your response to the insensitive remark is to say nothing "silence"… the sound of crickets.

What Could It All Mean?

In the presence of the crass, unbelievably poor behavior of others, it is often best to say nothing. If your stance of silence does not shake him out of his "fog of negativity," nothing will. You should, however, be aware that with this person, everyone gets an opportunity to be maligned. It is important to recognize that this is a person likely to speak negatively about you when it suits his purpose. Though you have rightly been protective of him during his vulnerable periods, nothing will protect you when he turns on you. Expect it and choose to maintain your dignity at all times. It is the law of nature that those who exude negative energy are likely to receive that type of energy in return, whether they are aware of it or not.

(Please refer to EEO practice guidelines for further information regarding this item.)

Line 17:
I Wish You And Your Family Well At This Time And Am Sorry For Your Loss.

17. The Line:

"I Wish You And Your Family Well At This Time And Am Sorry For Your Loss."

The Scene:

One of your team members has a dog she loves dearly. She spends a significant amount of time with and money on the dog and speaks of the dog in human terms. It is clear that the dog is a very important part of the person's family. Tragically, the dog passes away and your team member is overwrought and tearful about the loss. You say, "I wish you and your family well at this time and am sorry for your loss."

What Could It All Mean?

It is important to acknowledge what others care about—family, parents, children, pets. Never discount the impact of their losses. Do allow some discussion of the pet and, even if you do not like animals, do express condolences. Do not engage in jokes that might be considered cruel and in poor taste and may be hurtful to the pet owner.

Line 18:

YOU Do Have CHOICES.

18. The Line:

"YOU Do Have CHOICES."

The Scene:

A disgruntled, professionally licensed worker is leaving your organization. As part of his separation from the organization, an audit of his paperwork is conducted by his supervisor. It is discovered that there are significant deficiencies that would make the organization at risk for loss of certification. The worker is advised that further payment will be withheld pending completion of required paperwork. The worker marches into your office and threatens to report the organization on the basis of payment denied. You reply, "You do have choices."

What Could It All Mean?

The appropriate management of unhappy workers is critical to the success of an organization. In this instance, you should remind the worker that the failure to complete his work can be reported to the professional licensing entity for his state. The ramifications of this should be obvious. It is his choice to pursue his pay without the paperwork, though he is likely to have difficulty supporting the notion that he should be paid in full in the absence of completing his work. The message being sent is that he can choose to be professional, complete his work, be paid and move on or he can choose to initiate a fight that will result in possibly affecting his ability to work.

This situation also suggests the need for the organization to review how timely paperwork completion is monitored. Where possible, it is best to have systems in place that will alert supervisors as to when there are lapses before the point at which a staff person is leaving. This is so important an issue that some organizations hire people whose function is to monitor completion and quality of paperwork. Computerization of written document submission can also go a long way to improve compliance. As well, supervisors should conduct spot checks of paperwork so that issues can be addressed in the supervisory session. Newly hired staff should be closely monitored in the completion of written work so that there is a clear awareness that the organization requires compliance.

Line 19:
Let's Discuss It Over Coffee, Tea, Or Lunch.

"Let's Discuss It Over Coffee, Tea, Or Lunch."

The Scene:

You've hired a specialized professional for a critical role on your staff. He satisfies all of the criteria determined to be needed for the position. After three months in the position, you notice that he appears to have lost perspective. He is losing his temper with colleagues, making inappropriate demands, and requiring a significant amount of attention from everyone. You know that this represents a dramatic change in his behavior and may represent a stress in his life you know nothing about. Because of his high level within the organization, his behavior greatly affects the function of many. You meet with him and inform him of your concern about his recent behavior. He is embarrassed and almost tearful. You say to him, "Let's discuss it over coffee."

At the coffee, away from the organization, he explains that he has learned he is deeply in debt due to government student loans and that he is being required to move to a remote area of the country to repay the loans. He explains that he is overwhelmed by his responsibilities as a single parent and is concerned about the impact such a move will have on his child. He expresses the recognition that his behavior has changed and that he is having a negative impact upon the organization's function. The two of you are then able to develop a timeline for his seeking legal assistance, deciding on his course of action regarding his move, and ultimately for his continuing in his current position. In the coming months, his behavior improves dramatically though he ultimately decides to leave the position citing his need to significantly reduce the stress he is experiencing.

What Could It All Mean?

Sometimes an explosive situation can be diffused by offering a staff person the opportunity to say what is wrong without losing face within the organization. Used carefully, a conversation away from the site can lead to a greater degree of honesty and a higher level of problem solving. In the aforementioned scenario, the professional whose behavior is in question may feel less vulnerable discussing issues affecting his performance in a location away from the office. This type of intervention should be used when your relationship with the individual in question is such that neither party will feel compromised. It should not be overused and should be time limited as might be offered by coffee, tea, or lunch. Otherwise, this technique can lead to over familiarity resulting in you losing your credibility.

Line 20:
If This Continues, I Will Have No Recourse...

"Your Credentials YOU Promised ME!!!"

20. The Line:

"If This Continues, I Will Have No Recourse..."

The Scene:

You've hired a staff person in a position that requires a particular degree. She proves to be an excellent worker who develops wonderful rapport with all those she encounters. In a recent audit of your program, you learn that the required copy of the person's degree is not on file. You approach your staff member and remind her that you need the document. For the next three months she provides a variety of excuses as to why she has not produced the document. You finally say, "If this continues, I will have no recourse but to make a negative decision about your employment." She continues to avoid your requests and you call her educational institution only to find that she is several credits short of her degree. Despite her excellent work, you terminate her employment.

What Could It All Mean?

Unfortunately, people often feel "no one will find out" about serious lapses in the information they have provided in their resume. In this instance, had the staff person been honest, you might have been able to employ her at a different level while she completed the required credits. As a result of her dishonesty, she now is without a job and without your continued support. Your delay in verifying her documents has cost you precious time in that you will now have to train another person. As a person in charge of a program, your best bet is to verify necessary credentials as early in the employment process as possible.

Line 21:

Your Next Vacation Is Scheduled For When?

21. The Line

"Your Next Vacation Is Scheduled For When?"

The Scene:

A staff member has been at the top of his game in the office for more than 10 months. He is at the highest level of productivity in the organization and has been consistent in that regard. He does not complain or unnecessarily burden others, and handles all issues pertaining to his area with great effectiveness. Lately, he has been coming to work looking tired and seemingly "out of sorts." Usually jovial, he is pensive and has recently been sick twice within a four-week period. He has not even been willing to take adequate time off for illness. On each occasion of illness, he works from home for that day and returns to work still not feeling totally up to par. You meet with him and in the course of your discussion you say, "Your next vacation is scheduled for when?"

What Could It All Mean?

It is so important to recognize and to help your supervisees recognize when they are in danger of "burning out." It is also important to recognize the signs in ourselves. The pressure to be productive and our "24/7" technology have encouraged all of us to work around the clock and to set no limits pertaining to having a personal life or taking a vacation. The greatest leaders encourage their staff members to get appropriate rest, to work hard and smart, with strategy, and to take time for refueling. With this approach you establish your evaluation of the staff person's needs and your knowledge that working until the person collapses is not the best way. As well, this introduces the opportunity to review work flow and to ensure that the breadth of your staff member's responsibilities is appropriate, that he has the necessary assistance to get the job done, and/or that the work has been properly scheduled. Respect and concern for your reports goes a long way toward keeping energy and focus high in the work place.

Line 22:
Your Employment Has Been
TERMINATED.

"Your Employment Has Been TERMINATED."

The Scene:

You have hired someone who worked with you previously at another organization. You had no difficulties with this person but heard that the person left the other organization under vague circumstances. In discussions with him during the hiring process, he refers to having been disrespected at the previous organization. You have misgivings but, desperate to fill the critical position for which he is perfectly qualified, you hire him. At the same time you warn him that you will not be supportive if he discharges his responsibilities unprofessionally. Within two months, the person develops "family problems," first claiming to have family members who are critically ill and ultimately indicating he is involved in a legal matter that requires travel to another country. At the same time, he has developed conflicts with the manager to whom he reports and he begins to miss days at work without calling in or calling in and leaving messages at times when no one is available to speak to him. On one occasion, you reach him on his cell phone and he pretends that he cannot hear you. In the background, you hear music similar to that found in a shopping mall and beeping as the barcodes on items being purchased are swiped at the checkout counter. A day later, he calls you at a time he expects you to be unavailable and gets you directly. He tells you a long story about how he knows you have tried to reach him by mail, but that he has not read the mail. He indicates he is afraid to go to his home because he is being investigated by "Interpol." Remember the travel to another country? You request that he come in to discuss the issue. He insists he can come but it must be at the end of the work day. You agree to a meeting and, of course, he does not show. You mail a letter which includes the line, "Your employment has been terminated."

What Could It All Mean?

There are times when the truth is at least as strange as fiction. There are some people who seek employment and develop incredible stories to excuse unprofessional behavior. This is another instance in which clear and decisive action should be taken as you move to cut your losses. At least three valuable lessons become clear with this situation. The first is that when you hire in desperation, you often get a less than optimal outcome. Be prepared to act on the matter quickly. The second is that when people who you trust provide a neutral or negative assessment about an employee, do anticipate that things may not work out and be clear about your stance on the matter. The third lesson is that situations like this should not make you lose faith in human nature. Generally, the truth about troubled employees will surface quickly if appropriate levels of supervision are in place. It is not necessary to treat every employee with suspicion because of bad experiences with a few.

Line 23:

Actually...
NO!

"And Then After You Complete That 100 Item List, Do item 101..."

23. The Line:

"Actually...NO."

The Scene:

One of your managers makes a request of your executive assistant for information regarding the vacation time balance for a member of his staff. Your assistant sends the manager the information and cc's the staff person as has been the general policy in the past. The manager fires back a memo, cc'd to you, reprimanding your assistant for having cc'd the staff person and indicating that he would have preferred to share that information with the staff person. You send and e-mail to the manager indicating that it would be most productive if his requests are accompanied by specifics as to his wishes. The manager e-mails back, "Is it possible for her to remember that I prefer that information not be simultaneously sent to staff when I make a request?" You reply, "Actually…no". You further explain that requests should be accompanied by specific additional instructions making it unnecessary for anyone to have to remember the requirements of individual managers.

What Could It All Mean?

Sometimes persons in supervisory positions are disrespectful and/or dismissive of the crucial role played by "assistants" of all variety. They can feel that such a person is "just a secretary" (in this instance) and that they are in a role superior to that of your assistant. Hence, they may feel they have the right to be directive with <u>your</u> assistant. Your line and further direction clarify both issues from your perspective. You have modeled the manner in which you view members of your team and have not disrespected the manager in the process.

Line 24:

Get Over It!

"It's All Your Fault!!!"

24. The Line:

"Get Over It!"

The Scene

You have been invited to a meeting with a person regarding a serious issue within the organization. The person has concluded (without full information) that the issue has been caused by one individual. This person is rude and verbally abusive to the accused individual and to you. She cuts you and your staff off when speaking, allowing no real discussion. She repeatedly talks about her anger about the situation. She even goes so far as to indicate that her anger precluded her extending a party invitation to you. She continues to rant and rave about the history of the situation as she sees it. You finally say "Get over it!"

What Could It All Mean?

When a serious situation emerges at an organization, so too emerge opportunities to observe those who might be defined as "energy robbers." These are individuals who, when others are under stress or in a weakened position, seize the opportunity to "grind them into the ground." They are lacking in grace and usually do not feel a sense of real strength within themselves, particularly when facing other emotionally strong individuals, and so they seek to sap the energy of others they perceive to be weakened. In a social situation, you might seek to avoid or support this person, to help them feel strengthened so that they will cease the attack. On the contrary, in a business situation, when your staff may be subject to the attack, you must step in to stop the offending individual. Allowing them to continue to release unbridled anger is simply not productive. Your statement may snap them out of their stance. If it does not, this may be the time to discontinue the meeting, suggesting continuing when a more productive climate can prevail.

Line 25:
Stay In Your Lane.

25. The Line:

"Stay In Your Lane."

The Scene:

One of your directors determines that she is the arbiter of all that is correct and good. She has also assigned herself to identify everything she feels is wrong with the organization. Instead of working her concerns through the regular supervisory process, she has even been inappropriately allowed to share said information with people she believes have the power to advance her position. What is striking about her actions is her complete lack of innovation or development of energy with respect to the program she runs despite having been given every resource and opportunity to build it. She has been supervised and supported on developing her program and has been allowed to share her "concerns." In an ultimate attempt to get more attention, she arrives at your door to give more unsolicited insight into improvements that can be made beyond her program. You say, "Stay in your lane."

What Could It All Mean?

There are those in organizations who spend a great deal of time identifying the faults of others rather than focusing on ways in which they can improve the organization through their own actions. They are in "the lanes" of others on a regular basis. They generally function best within the tiny worlds they have developed for themselves. This enables them to achieve "perfection" in their world since they never take the chance that would be required to try something new. They are among the most insidious within an organization because they operate behind the scenes to dismantle the efforts of others. They also seek to seize every opportunity for attention despite their own mediocrity. Managing people like this can be difficult because their negative actions can often escape the light until they have done serious damage. The one effective way to counteract this type of person is to provide "tight" supervision and to document their lack of movement within their own program. Your line seeks to refocus them on their "lane." Unfortunately, there is little that can be done should they join forces with other negative forces. Ultimately, if it is the will of those "in power" to maintain a petty, "small world" view, those with a more expansive view may need to decide whether this environment is the right one for them.

Line 26:

BRING IT ON!

26. The Line:

"BRING IT ON."

The Scene:

You run an organization that provides services to vulnerable people. One of your management team members informs you that a staff person has been verbally abusive in a sexually suggestive manner toward one of the organization's clients. When questioned about the situation, the staff person admits to the behavior, is unapologetic and cavalier, even suggesting that this behavior might be entertaining to the client. You are appalled and recommend, following a check with the organization's lawyer, that the staff person be dismissed. Your management team member carries out the action and then is threatened with legal action by the offending staff person. You say, "Bring it on."

What Could It All Mean?

There does come a point when you must take the "bull by the horns" with respect to unacceptable behavior by staff. In this instance, swift, decisive action is the only appropriate choice. Not only was the behavior disrespectful, abusive, and demeaning to the client, but it placed the organization at risk of a law suit. Additionally, it is likely that this may not have been the first instance of this behavior, and without intervention, would not have been the last. Furthermore, other staff members, likely aware of the behavior, need to witness the clear and focused management of the situation. Once the legal parameters have been checked, managers should not back off because of threats of legal action.

Line 27:

"I've Stayed TOO LONG At The Fair."

27. The Line:

"I've Stayed TOO LONG At The Fair."

The Scene:

You've been hired by a limitedly financed organization to help it evolve. You joined the organization, particularly because you believed in its mission. You've been asked to market it, develop it, upgrade it, etc. You do so, yet the corporate team that should assist you resists doing their part and passively watches you doing the heavy lifting. You persist with your efforts and you try to engage them in the process. You show by example, you develop products exemplifying what is needed; you bring in experts to support the need for their particular input. You even succeed in having others join the effort but find that they fade away, observing that the team is offering no energy for what truly needs to be done. Ultimately, the organization's lack of fiscal reserves wears on its foundation and the organization is faced with serious financial difficulties. At this point, the passive team comes alive to point fingers and lay blame at your door. You are in disbelief, but come to realize that the team members are now out to grandstand and save face. After you take some time to analyze what has happened, you recognize that your efforts to "bring the team along" were to no avail. You say, "I've stayed too long at the fair," participate in an orderly transition for the organization and go on to do other things.

What Could It All Mean?

Leaders who are innovative, committed, and multitalented in many instances encounter work situations in which those to whom they report will let them "do it all." While things are going well, and despite the wear and tear on the leader, there may be verbal praise, etc. in the absence of a real team approach to solving the organization's problems. "Can do" leaders may tend to "carry" others along as they can see the potential for success and believe "if I can just get them to see what we can do," the passive group will get on board. The problem with this approach is that the leaders stand alone, as they have all along, when criticism starts to fly. Hence, it is important for leaders to evaluate at the onset and throughout their tenure within an organization, whether they truly have a "team" working with them. Once leaders assess that the true support and effort of others needed to get the job done is lacking, they should truly develop an exit strategy. In the end, if they do not, a toxic environment may develop and they may end up being the ready target for others to place blame.

Line 28:

"Requiem For An Assassin..."

"Light Reading Anyone?"

28. The Line:

"Requiem For An Assassin... Light Reading Anyone?"

The Scene:

A meeting is called to discuss the dissolution of an organization due to financial insolvency. The series of events leading to this final action have been difficult and fraught with complicated, secretive, and often blatantly self-serving acts on the part of the governing body of the organization. Professionals have been unfairly slandered and mistreated. One of the persons attending the meeting brings a book he has been reading to the meeting and places it on the table. As each offending person enters the room, they look at the book, recoil in horror and hesitantly sit in chairs distant from the owner of the book. Finally, the book reader realizes why all are concerned and laughs as he reads the title out loud, "Requiem for an Assassin by Barry Eisler" following which he says, "Light reading anyone?" He follows his statement by explaining the premise of the fictional book about a CIA operative.

What Could It All Mean?

During tense times within the life of an organization, the most innocent of acts can be totally misinterpreted. In this instance, many of those who recoiled at the book title had been engaged in negative actions to which they were uncertain as to whether others might have responded with murderous impulses. There are two lessons central to this scene. The first is to be careful of what you might introduce to a situation that could make others fearful. In this instance, the book reader was able to break the ice and to explain that the book did not represent a threat to anyone. There might not have been an opportunity for explanation in another situation, however. Second, do be careful about the way in which you treat others under your employ. It is of the utmost importance that you abstain from unnecessary bashing, gossip, and innuendo even if you feel the person has earned your ire. You do not want to be on the receiving end of real threats to your safety.

Line 29:
"In The End, The TRUTH Will Come Out."

29. The Line:

"In The End, The TRUTH Will Come Out."

The Scene:

A middle management person in the finance office of the organization allows herself to be seduced into "backstabbing" her supervisor. She shares confidential information with other middle managers and, though she was involved in and responsible for some fiscal errors that were made, absolves herself of responsibility, blaming everything on others. She takes credit for the work of others and, though she has been extremely difficult to work with and for, presents herself as the "only professional" member of her team. She succeeds in being chosen to replace her supervisor by an ill-informed governing body of the organization. Once she has accomplished this, she attempts to engage you in a discussion of the rationale for her actions. You decline the discussion and you say, "In the end, the truth will come out."

What Could It All Mean?

In today's precarious work environment in which it seems, "by any means necessary" is the way to get ahead, it might be tempting to join with or to be supportive of those who get ahead through acts that are lacking in ethics. Certainly, people who conduct themselves in this manner can seem to be "riding high in April" but they are often "shot down in May." Even in the absence of your witnessing their ultimate disappointment or failure, you must choose to be clear on your own ethics. Additionally, consider the fact that people who act in this way toward someone else may also choose to act in this way toward you.

BUY A SHARE OF THE FUTURE IN YOUR COMMUNITY

These certificates make great holiday, graduation and birthday gifts that can be personalized with the recipient's name. The cost of one S.H.A.R.E. or one square foot is $54.17. The personalized certificate is suitable for framing and will state the number of shares purchased and the amount of each share, as well as the recipient's name. The home that you participate in "building" will last for many years and will continue to grow in value.

Here is a sample SHARE certificate:

HABITAT FOR HUMANITY

THIS CERTIFIES THAT
YOUR NAME HERE
HAS INVESTED IN A HOME FOR A DESERVING FAMILY

1985-2005

TWENTY YEARS OF BUILDING FUTURES IN OUR
COMMUNITY ONE HOME AT A TIME

1200 SQUARE FOOT HOUSE @ $65,000 = $54.17 PER SQUARE FOOT
This certificate represents a tax-deductible donation. It has no cash value.

YES, I WOULD LIKE TO HELP!

I support the work that Habitat for Humanity does and I want to be part of the excitement! As a donor, I will receive periodic updates on your construction activities but, more importantly, I know my gift will help a family in our community realize the dream of homeownership. **I would like to SHARE in your efforts against substandard housing in my community!** *(Please print below)*

PLEASE SEND ME _____ SHARES at $54.17 EACH = $ $_____

In Honor Of: _____

Occasion: (Circle One)   *HOLIDAY*   *BIRTHDAY*   *ANNIVERSARY*

     OTHER: _____

Address of Recipient: _____

Gift From: _____ *Donor Address:* _____

Donor Email: _____

I AM ENCLOSING A CHECK FOR $ $_____ PAYABLE TO HABITAT FOR HUMANITY **OR** PLEASE CHARGE MY VISA OR MASTERCARD *(CIRCLE ONE)*

Card Number _____ Expiration Date: _____

Name as it appears on Credit Card _____ Charge Amount $ _____

Signature _____

Billing Address _____

Telephone # Day _____ Eve _____

PLEASE NOTE: Your contribution is tax-deductible to the fullest extent allowed by law.
Habitat for Humanity • P.O. Box 1443 • Newport News, VA 23601 • 757-596-5553
www.HelpHabitatforHumanity.org

Printed in the USA
CPSIA information can be obtained
at www.ICGtesting.com
JSHW082220140824
68134JS00015B/639